Next Time I Move, They'll
Carry Me Out in a Box

Melanie

Thanks for the great
opportunity on WBAL!
You rock!!!!

Warmly,

Noj

ADVANCE PRAISE FOR

Next Time I Move, They'll Carry Me Out in a Box

"Michele Wojciechowski is a humor writer who writes actual humor, and a living human who lives like a real human, with broken appliances, a house that grows dirt, and a husband who needs psychological counseling. You're going to love her misadventures, but most of all you're going to love how she finds the funny in the things that drive us all a little crazy."

--W. Bruce Cameron, author of the New York Times bestsellers *8 Simple Rules for Dating My Teenage Daughter* and *A Dog's Purpose* as well as its sequel, *A Dog's Journey*

"Anyone who's selling a home or considering it will enjoy the humor and candor in *Next Time I Move, They'll Carry Me Out in a Box*. One part group therapy and one part roadmap, this is a home-sellers manual without the snooze factor. The tone in this very relatable book is just right for any homeowner who wants nothing more than to see a 'sold' sign in their front yard and to move on to their next home without incident or injury."

--Margaret Kelly, Chief Executive Officer, RE/MAX LLC

"I didn't think there was anything funny about moving. Until I read Michele Wojciechowski's laugh-until-you-cry essays on the subject, that is. One thing is for sure, if I ever decide to move, I won't let the appliances overhear."

--Nancie Clare, Editor-in-Chief,
Los Angeles Times Magazine

"In this collection of essays about her and her husband's hasty move from one house to another, witty and perceptive author Michele 'Wojo' Wojciechowski manages to turn the whole frustrating ordeal into a marvelous romp that's engaging, entertaining, and flat-out funny."

--Rick Detorie, Nationally Syndicated Cartoonist of "One Big Happy" and award-winning author of
The Accidental Genius of Weasel High

"The hilarity of home buying and selling is rich real estate in *Next Time I Move, They'll Carry Me Out in a Box*. The American Dream can be a comedy of nightmares. Location, location, location, you want to be with Wojo when she raises her eyebrows (and her arms in supplication)."

--Suzette Martinez Standring, Syndicated Columnist and award-winning author, *The Art of Column Writing*

"If you're moving, thinking of moving, or have moved, *Next Time I Move, They'll Carry Me Out in a Box* is the perfect salve for your aches and pains. Read it when you're hiding at the coffee shop during your Open House."

--Jen Singer, author of *You're a Good Mom (And Your Kids Aren't So Bad Either)*

"Michele Wojciechowski's new book, *Next Time I Move, They'll Carry Me Out in a Box* is a must read for anyone who has ever dreamed of moving into a new home. Her laugh-out-loud account of her relocation nightmare will quickly change your mind…and you will never look at bubble wrap the same way again!"

--Tracy Beckerman, syndicated humor columnist and author of *Rebel without a Minivan: Observations on Life in the 'Burbs*

"*Next Time I Move, They'll Carry Me Out in a Box* is like group therapy for anyone buying a house, selling a house, or making a move! Don't let this book get packed away– you'll want to keep it close by for regular doses of smiles!"

--Jim Higley, columnist and author of *Bobblehead Dad: 25 Life Lessons I Forgot I Knew*

"What do you do when your appliances revolt, the walls of your home buckle, and your husband suddenly becomes possessed by Mr. Clean? Well, if you're Michele Wojciechowski, you turn it into comedy gold. Her latest book, *Next Time I Move, They'll Carry Me Out in a Box* is a laugh-out-loud romp through home ownership and upgrade. You'll laugh through every appliance in the throes of a prolonged demise, every mislabeled moving box, and each and every bit of marital anxiety that home ownership brings.

"*Next Time I Move, They'll Carry Me Out in a Box* is so good that it should not only be pleasurable reading, it also should be required reading for anyone who is even thinking of buying a home. If it were, two things would be certain: we'd have a lot more laughers and a lot more renters."

--James Mendrinos, author of *The Complete Idiot's Guide to Comedy Writing*

"Michele Wojciechowski is the kind of warm, charming writer you want to spend an afternoon with. If you're thinking about moving, read this book instead. It'll be way more fun. (And cheaper.)"

--Jenny Hagel, Comedy Writer, (MTV, VH1, Second City)

Next Time I Move, They'll Carry Me Out in a Box

Michele Wojciechowski

Next Time I Move, They'll Carry Me Out in a Box
Copyright © 2012 Michele Wojciechowski.
All rights reserved.

Published by Wojo Enterprises, LLC, Kingsville, MD 21087.
www.WojosWorld.com

First Edition

Cover Illustration: Tom Chalkley, www.tomchalk.com;
Suzanne Grover, www.groverartwork.com
Layout Design: Caitlin Proctor, www.designcatstudio.com

Library of Congress Control Number: 2012914666

ISBN-13: 978-0-9881893-0-0
ISBN-10: 0988189305

Dedication

For my Mom, who always believed in me. For my Dad, who was such a funny guy. For both of you, I miss you every day. Thanks for passing down your great senses of humor. For Ed, who keeps me smiling every day.

For Brad, my husband and partner in crime, thanks for always being there. And for helping me laugh, even when I wanted to cry. We're never moving again!

Contents

Acknowledgments

Just like they did when I moved, lots of folks helped me along the way while I wrote this book. Thanks to Sandy Smith, Super Realtor, for being so good to us and for not killing me even when she may have wanted to.

To the amazing Robin Blakely; you believed in this book from the start...and in me. I am blessed to call you friend.

Thanks to Sandra Hume, a great editor, who brought up a problem with "tense," and for once, it didn't mean I was too stressed out. To Tom Chalkley, who so brilliantly captured me in a cartoon, and to Suzanne Grover, who took it to the next level.

Thanks to Jen Singer, Fred Minnick, and Ron Doyle for reading the earliest draft. Thanks to all the readers of Wojo's World™, who followed this story as it happened and laughed a lot.

To Andrea King Collier, Dara Chadwick, Lisa Iannucci, and Margaret Gilmour—thank you for helping me get through.

To Julia Mattis, thanks for teaching me so much and for your friendship.

Thanks to Kathie, Lori, Cellina, Danielle, Leslie, Julie, and Fr. Tim Brown for keeping me sane.

Rosie, thank you for being such a great friend and for keeping me from throwing my computer out the window. Thanks also for reading this many, many times.

Ernie, thanks for being a great friend and for listening to me read this out loud over and over and over again.

Thanks to my late parents Bev and Len; you taught me how to find the funny in life, and I will be forever grateful. Thanks to Ed; you're the happiest man I've ever met.

Finally, to Brad, you always believed in me, even when I had no idea how I would make a career out of writing. And here we are—still laughing every single day...

FOREWORD

Five years ago, I had the distinct pleasure of being Michele "Wojo" Wojciechowski's real estate agent when she had her "epiphany" while out driving and found her dream home. Michele is a special person, client, and now personal friend. She dreams big dreams, lives life large, loves like there's no tomorrow, and dedicates herself to making others' lives even sweeter.

Did I also mention that she's hilarious? I've been a real estate agent for 10 years and honestly will tell you that clients are, well, sometimes just clients. Michele is different.

Michele is such a good writer because she loves to learn. She pays attention and brings her bold personality and unique perspective to everything she does. She is so creative that her imagination allows her to reach for things others would consider unobtainable. You can hear her laugh from across the room, and it causes you to smile. When she cries, you feel the pain with her. That's just the way she touches your heart!

I admit that I didn't quite "get" Michele at first. She found a home that she fell in love with from the outside, and we went to see the inside together. We walked through the house with the seller at our heels. Michele spoke out loud as we went from room to room. She loved it, she knew she had to have it, and she was willing to leave it up to me to help her find a way to make it happen. We ultimately did.

Did I mention the seller was walking through the house with us? Didn't leave much room for me to negotiate, did it?

This is Michele. When she sets her sights on something, there is nothing that will get in her way. That's what made her such a great seller. Michele was willing to do whatever I told her to get her home sold (while most folks may not) so that she and her husband could buy their dream home.

I was like a drill sergeant: "Pack it up, put it away, move it out. Put the toilet lid down, hide it under the bed, stick it in the oven." She happily did it all.

Some experts say buying and selling real estate is one of the most stressful things we do in our lifetime.

So expect some tears, some anger, and maybe even a little yelling. But in the end, the laughter will carry you through.

Michele knew what her dream was, found humor in the process, and lived to tell about it in this fun-loving book about the adventures she experienced. If you want some advice, read on. You'll learn some things and have a laugh because we can all see ourselves in these stories.

Chase your dream. Life is short. Use the good china and the nice linens. And don't spend too much time worrying about the dust, because there will always be more!

--Sandy Smith, ABR, GREEN,
RE/MAX American Dream

We're Thinking of Moving, and Our Home Has Found Out

Years ago, Brad (my husband) and I took a home improvement class through a local continuing education program. Our teacher, who had been a plumber and contractor for years, said to us early on, "You have to remember that your house is a living thing. It moves, it shifts, it breathes…"

At the time, I thought, "Yeah, right. The walls have ears."

The scary thing is that now I think they do.

For the last year, we've been talking about moving. We want to stay in the same area, just in a bigger house. Our needs have changed, and we want more space.

This seems logical to us.

Our house, however, has other ideas.

We've owned our current home for more than 11 years. We like it; it likes us. That's how it's been. Repairs are usually relatively minor. Everyone gets along.

Well, the house must be listening closely because it's found out that we're planning a move. How do I know this? It's starting to ruin things, and I think it's out of spite.

It all began with the dishwasher. Granted, our dishwasher was really old (as in God said, "Let there be light," then created our dishwasher). We knew we were living with it on borrowed time. We decided to replace it when it began to, um, forget to clean the glasses completely.

This wasn't too upsetting, though, because we had planned on replacing it; we got a great deal on a new one, and this really wasn't the end of the world.

Until the other appliances began to follow suit.

After returning from a business trip with a few suit-cases filled with dirty clothes, I went to the basement to do some laundry.

The washing machine was having none of this.

Great.

The next morning, I called a repair company that was able to send a man out pretty quickly. It was our timer, he said. When he gave me the quote to fix it, my husband and I decided that it would make more sense to just replace it. Which we did.

We were happy. We had really clean dishes from our nice, new dishwasher, and the clothes, well, it was just nice to be able to wash clothes again and get rid of the mountains of textiles that had accumulated in the basement.

But then the stove joined in.

Okay, this was getting ridiculous.

One of the burners on our stove began to not work. Then it would work. Then not. It was taunting us—was the dang thing broken or just playing a practical joke?

No joke. It broke.

Luckily—and I know this is the only time in my life when this has actually happened—we had a service policy on it, which didn't expire for two whole months.

Usually, when something breaks, it happens a mere few days after the policy has already expired. So in this case, I was thrilled.

Service man came. Replaced some wires. Stove was now fixed.

Whew, I thought, thank goodness this is all over.

The house, though, had other plans.

During a torrential downpour, where we got something like 700 inches of rain in about 10 minutes, we got water in our basement—for the first time in nearly seven years.

When this initially happened, we called in a professional, did everything he said, and life was good. No more water. No more leaks.

But our house is ticked and not afraid to show it.

So over the next few days, we'll be visited by contractors and repair people who will help us fix everything up right.

I hope the house is finished with its temper tantrum. I'm praying it's gotten everything out of its system.

If it hasn't, I hate to see what might happen when we actually begin making solid plans to move.

If we go to an Open House and our home finds out, what will it do? Will we return home to find a burst pipe?

A leaky roof?

An exploded toilet?

And while it may seem that an exploded toilet couldn't happen, I really don't know my home anymore and what it's capable of doing.

Especially in my absence.

You know what? I really don't want to know either.

I have to admit, though, that I've begun talking really nicely to the refrigerator and the air conditioning unit.

Because you just never know.

Buying a House Is More Than Just Location, Location, Location

My husband and I have begun looking for a new home.

Well, let me rephrase that. We're *sort of* looking for a new home.

But it's not like we're *seriously* looking yet. We've just been poking around.

So, for example, if this were a dating-type situation, we would be playing the field. No engagement ring. No date set. Just checking out what's on the market, but not making any kind of commitment.

(You hear that, home? We're not leaving. So don't break anything else!)

In the relatively short time that we have been looking around, though, we have learned a lot.

A whole lot.

Actually, we've learned way more than any couple should ever know about what people do—or don't do—when selling their homes.

I've decided that for the good of the community, my country, and the world at large, I will share some of these things with you so that you may learn from our experiences.

To people selling your homes: there are just a few simple things you can do to make your home much more appealing to buyers. Uh, like CLEAN IT!

I'm serious. You would not believe the number of people who do not clean their homes before an Open House. And I'm not saying that a house has to pass the white glove test done on the very top of the cabinets. It would be nice, though, if people thought to—oh, I don't know—perhaps scrub the toilet and clean the bathtub.

Seeing the ring in your tub doesn't make me want to run right out and put in a contract. Really. Get some of those talking bubble guys and a sponge. It's not that difficult.

Also, if you're selling your home and your carpet is full of pet urine stains from your incontinent dog or your new puppy, again, GET THIS CLEANED! I have no desire to shell out tons of my hard-earned cash to buy your house that has stinky, icky urine stains.

This is high on the "Yuck" list. Trust me on this.

If you have dogs, and they stink, give them baths. If your cats are smelling up the place, change the litter. Get some air freshener! I don't want to smell your cats' pee.

(Or poo, for that matter. You get the point.)

While I'm talking about pets, if you have pets other than fish, please take them out of the house when it's being shown. Why? Because some people, who are, uh, not me of course, could be afraid of cats, even just a little bit. And if you have two or three cats, I think it would be an even better idea to take them all out of the house so that I, I mean other people, don't have heart attacks when they suddenly feel like they are in a Stephen King flick and have just gotten to the part where the innocent couple looking at the nice house is attacked by the posse of strange, scary cats. (Coming soon to a theater near you, *The Day the Cats Attacked!*)

I haven't even had an Open House at my home yet, and I already know that when you show your home, you should put away all personal items—like family photos, framed diplomas, etc.

Personal stuff like this doesn't bother me. Really. I can envision myself somewhere even if Johnny's diploma is on the wall or Sally's award is on a bookcase. In fact, I'd think that was pretty cool.

Unless, of course, the personal stuff is a little *too* personal—like that dirty underwear you've left on the floor of your walk-in closet. Hello? It's a "walk-in" closet. This means that when I'm looking at your house, I'm going to walk into it. It's true. I will.

You can stuff the dirty laundry into the washing machine if you want; I'm not picky about where you put it, and I won't be looking in there anyway. But if it's right on the floor in front of me, well, see the "Yuck" factor above.

If you have wallpaper, and there's a big, honking water stain on it, be sure to tell your real estate agent why it's there. If you've had a leak, is it fixed? Because it doesn't make me feel good to ask and have the agent brush it off and say, "Oh, I don't know what happened, but if it's anything big, it will show up in the home inspection."

Oh. Okay. So let me get this straight. You want me to fall in love with your house, put in a contract, put my house up for sale, and then wait to see if everything works out in the home inspection, only to find out that due to a leak, there is a pond forming under the basement and the whole place is filled with mold.

I get it. Okey dokey.

One final thought: please make sure that—if you want to sell your home to anyone but college kids—it doesn't look like a frat house. One home we viewed did.

Every room on the first floor, except for the kitchen, had couches in it.

Every. Single. One.

In the dining room, there was what I guess was something pretending to be a dining room table. But you really couldn't tell because it was surrounded by couches.

And they weren't exactly clean couches either…

While looking at one home, we were told to ignore the mess in the backyard, as the owner had had a party the night before.

No duh. Couldn't tell that by all the crushed beer cans lying around on the grass. And the tons of cigarette butts in the mulch. Oh yeah, and the charred remnants of last night's bonfire.

None of this was an immediate tip-off. Nope. Not at all.

Remember that whole "cleaning your house" thing I mentioned above? That includes the yard. Including doggie doo or beer cans or anything else stinky or yucky that I really don't want to see.

Thanks. See you next Sunday.

Maybe New? Maybe Not...

After going to several Open Houses on our own, my husband and I wanted to shake things up a bit.

We decided to look at a couple of not-yet-built communities in the area where we might want to live. Just to see if that would suit us better.

First, let me say that I'm sure not all home builders are like the ones I'm going to talk about, who shall remain nameless. In fact, I know they aren't, because close family members and friends of ours have had their homes built. They picked out land, chose a style of home, and selected all the fun extras.

I even know that this can be a *good* experience.

Unfortunately, for the hubby and me, the non-existent homes remain that way for us—non-existent.

Why? Oh, the reasons seem endless...

But let me share a few with you.

At one place, we met with someone in a trailer. I had no problem with this, as I've been in some really nice trailers in my day.

This one wasn't.

The guy showed us the house choices through blueprints.

But I'm not an architect.

Or a draftsman.

Or even a bank robber…

So showing me blueprints and expecting me to be able to visualize the resulting home is kind of like giving me *A Tale of Two Cities* written in Swahili, and then asking me to talk about the wonderful prose.

It's not gonna happen because I just don't get it.

There are some things that you accept in life without seeing them first.

Babies, for instance…

You know whether you married a George Clooney or Charlize Theron lookalike–or someone who resembles the Hunchback of Notre Dame. So you have an idea of what your baby might look like.

Let's face it—no matter what, you're going to love your baby.

You don't do the same thing with a house. Especially one that you've only seen in blueprints.

Show me photos, at least. Take me into a model home. Isn't that how you do this?

But, no. We sat in a crappy trailer looking at blueprints.

And then we left.

Next up was a development to be built. The sign touted that the houses started at a price that was well below our price cap.

We were excited.

We were thrilled.

We were stupid.

It turns out, that with this company, practically everything was an "extra." This means you have to pay more for it. A lot more.

Want a roof?

A door?

Some windows?

A floor?

Extra!!!

Okay, not all of that was extra. But bay windows? Extra! Sinks that actually look like they came from *Better Homes and Gardens* rather than the dump? Extra! Carpet that was better than the old remnant you use in the garage when you change your oil? Extra!

By the time we got everything we wanted written up with the sales rep, we had gone an "extra" $180,000 over the "houses starting at" price.

And, trust me; we weren't selecting gold toilets and cashmere carpeting.

The final place we contacted also hadn't been built, but we could view a model at another location.

We did.

The house was actually nice. Problem was that the only lots left in the development were near some kind of water drainage system.

"Um, so will there be standing water if it rains?" I asked.

The sales guy said he wasn't sure. The houses hadn't been built yet.

"If there is, will you drain it?"

He couldn't comment on it because he didn't know if they would need to.

Perhaps this scenario seems normal to some folks. Perhaps they would even go ahead and buy the house. But all I kept imagining was my husband and me sitting outside with our guests for our first cookout, held after a long series of rain storms.

And standing water.

And tons and tons of mosquitoes.

We passed.

Because if I wanted to live in the wetlands, I would move to the Everglades.

Your Dream Home Is What Happens to You When You're Busy Making Other Plans

While it's true that my husband and I have been looking for a home, we haven't really been doing what I would call *looking* looking.

You know what I mean. Like when you're in grade school, and your friend says, "Do you like Billy?" And you respond, "Well, I like him, but I don't *like him* like him."

We've scoped out some of the homes that are on the market, but we haven't gotten serious.

No commitments. Not even close.

We've been playing the field, waiting for Mr. Right— or in this case, Mr. Right House.

Brad and I want our next home to be our last. We've compiled a list of "must haves" for this home, and Sandy, our Realtor, has sent us links to homes that fulfill our criteria.

After my mom passed away, we decided that my stepdad would live with us. He was 14 years older than my mom, and we don't want him to be all by himself. So, we want our new home to have a first-floor bed and bath. That way, as he gets older, if he has problems with stairs, he can remain on the first floor.

In the area of Baltimore where we are looking, we would have better luck getting an open table in a fancy restaurant on Valentine's Day.

But it's on the list, so we need to have it.

I want a front porch. My husband wants a garage, preferably a two-car one located on the side of the house. But he will settle for any garage, period.

We both want a gas stove and gas or oil heat.

We aren't asking for much. We just want what we want.

That is, if we can ever find it...

One weekend in January, Brad and I went to a bed and breakfast in Maryland because I was writing about it for a magazine. Before we left, I printed out another listing that Sandy had sent. It said it had an "in-law suite," but I didn't pay attention to this verbiage much anymore because it usually meant a bedroom, but nothing else.

Why they just don't call them "in-law bedrooms" I don't know. Probably because then they couldn't raise the purchase price.

Before we left to come home, we looked at the listing.

I was confused because when I looked at the photos of the house, there appeared to be two different kinds of kitchen cabinets in it.

"Why in the world would anyone have a kitchen with two different kinds of cabinets?" I asked my husband.

He was just as stumped as I.

Then I suddenly understood.

These people weren't decorating impaired. There were *two* kitchens in this house!

It had a "real" in-law suite…with its own kitchen.

And it was in our price range.

Gas stove, I mean stoves?

Check!

Gas heat?

Check!

And it also had a two-and-a-half-car garage. Where we would get another half of car, I didn't know, but my husband was pretty happy. Still, he was cautious.

We decided to take a look at the house from the outside for the heck of it because it was on our way home. We had nothing to lose.

I'll never forget Brad's reaction when we pulled up in front of the house.

He gasped. Out loud.

He never gasped at any of the other homes we looked at. But the others didn't have a front porch like this one.

Or a two-and-a-half-car garage—that loaded from the side of the house.

Or a yard, a really big yard.

We are so excited. We want to see this house right away.

We've called Sandy, and, so far, she hasn't been able to reach the homeowners.

How can we ever wait another day? We've finally found Mr. Right House!

If we were dating, we would spend the next 24 hours waiting for the phone to ring, for him to call…

Going Once, Going Twice, Going Three Times—Sold!

Our Realtor was able to get us in to see the house the very next evening. Which was good, because we were both so excited that I think we would have had apoplexy if we had to wait any longer.

I'm not good at the whole waiting thing. My husband usually is, but in this case, he was just as happily deranged as I was.

I got nothing worthwhile accomplished the entire day. Every so often, I'd begin to freak out, and I'd call my husband at work.

"I was just thinking," I'd say. "Suppose the house is a horrible mess inside."

"Michele, we saw photos of it," he'd reply. "It's not a mess."

"Well, suppose there is mold and broken plumbing, and we're getting excited over nothing," I said.

"Honey, they have to disclose that stuff," he answered. "It's okay to be excited."

"Suppose we can't get a loan? Suppose we go in tonight, and it's perfect and our total dream home, and then we get in touch with banks, and they laugh at us with their deep, bankery voices saying, 'We don't care how good your credit is, you're not getting this house!'?"

At this, my husband paused. I can only imagine the face he made before he spoke again.

"Michele, calm down. Everything is going to be okay. Suppose it *is* our dream home, and we *do* get a loan? Huh? Suppose that happens?"

Oh. My. God.

I hadn't thought of it that way. I'm so encouraging and optimistic when helping my friends. But when it comes to me and this kind of situation—a big, potentially good one—I begin to imagine that the Boogie Man of all Boogie Men is going to somehow come around and ruin it.

"Yeah, that could happen, too…" I trailed off.

"That's exactly what's going to happen," he said.

That night, Brad, my stepdad, and I went to see our potential House-Soul Mate.

It is what we dreamed of. Lots of bedrooms. Lots of bathrooms. And something else: an honest to-goodness in-law suite. My stepdad is going to have his own kitchen, living room, bedroom, and bathroom. Best of all, it is connected directly to our part of the house—our living room will be joined to his.

Yes, I have begun referring to it as "our" this and "our" that.

When we were in the car driving home, we asked my stepdad, who is usually not really demonstrative about stuff like this, what he thought about the house.

"That house is all right!" he exclaimed.

That's just what he did—exclaimed.

We knew it was the house for us.

But you know how you tend to freak out about major life events like this? Or rather, I do?

Brad and I decided that we wanted to see the house in the daytime. Just to make sure that the night hadn't hidden things.

And because all the "buying a home" books and websites tell you to do this.

And because we were afraid that we had been dreaming.

The next day, we saw the house again. It was just as wonderful as it had been before.

So did we go make an offer and sign a contract?

Nope. I was still freaking out.

I asked my Aunt Kathie and Uncle Tom to come from Pennsylvania to look at it. You know, just to make sure we hadn't missed anything.

They loved it as much as we did. "If I were you, and I could buy it, I would," said Aunt Kathie. This was a good thing because by this time, Brad and I were measuring spaces in the house to see if our kitchen table would fit, if our dining room table would fit, and if our bed would fit in the master bedroom.

"You know, Michele," our Realtor, Sandy, said, "You're making it really difficult for me to negotiate on this house for you."

Why? Just because we had seen the house three times in less than a week? Or because we were walking around measuring it?

Perhaps it was that we did these things while one of the homeowners was present. Guess wc weren't exactly being subtle.

After seeing the home in its entirety again, my husband and I went out to the front porch. We sat on the porch swing and began to gently move it.

I looked at the homeowner and said, "I've always wanted a front porch swing like this."

"You buy this house, and I'll leave it," he said. "But the deer heads on the wall in the basement are going with me."

Fine by me.

Not a problem, Mr. Homeowner. Not a problem at all.

We know what we want. This is it.

We're ready for the proposal.

Getting Your House
Ready for Sale Is an All-New
Kind of Hell

We've found our dream home! Life is great!

There's just one thing…according to our contract, we have to get our present house ready to be put on the market in a little over a week.

You heard me—in just over a week.

I'll pause. Let you take that in.

Look around your own home.

Go ahead. I'll wait.

Imagine having to get it all together to sell in 10 days.

Now you know how I feel.

I'm writing this on the day before our house is officially going on the market. And it will be ready. Of course, from all the stress, I will probably be eating Tums by the handfuls for the rest of my life to get rid of the indigestion.

I have one question to ask God, the Universe, or anyone else out there who will listen: Exactly how did I accumulate so much stuff?

I used to get on my late mom about that. She was a total packrat. Not *Hoarders* status, but a packrat. I, on the other hand, have been getting rid of things for years to combat the packratism that runs in my family.

I've decided that the stuff must be like rabbits—it must multiply when I go to sleep at night. Because there is no way that I brought all this stuff into our house.

And I've learned something: you don't realize just how much stuff you have until you begin to put it in boxes.

Tons and tons and tons of boxes…

What's funny, too, is that it suddenly becomes quite easy to get rid of things that wouldn't have been easy to part with, until you contemplate having to move it. Or pack it. Or store it.

We've filled trash bags galore. We've made trips to the dump. We've gotten together lots for charity.

And we've still got stuff.

I know that most of the stuff we own is either mine (as in, I brought it into this relationship) or belongs to both my husband and me.

That's how I was able to determine exactly how much stress I was under with all of this going on. I saw my husband getting together his three—count 'em, three—boxes of stuff that he had brought into our relationship.

And I went a bit ballistic.

"Do you really need all the stuff that's in those boxes?" I asked him.

He looked up at me with the "Are you really serious?" look.

I'm getting tired of this look.

I've been getting it a lot during the past week.

"I only have three boxes, and one of them is filled with my sports trophies," he said.

"Sports trophies? Do you really need all those cheap trophies with the little baseball player on the top? Really?"

"Hey, I've got one from when I played basketball in high school."

Every time my poor husband mentions having been on his high school basketball team, the only thing I can think of is the story he tells about the game in which he was so proud to score a basket…until he realized it was for the other team.

And, yes, I felt the need to bring this up.

Not exactly the smartest thing I've done lately.

"I was a good player!" he exclaimed. "That was a one-time thing."

He was on a roll. "And, I'm keeping every single trophy, and if I find more, I'm going to keep them too—even if I end up with four or five or six boxes! Because you have 7 billion boxes, and we still have stuff in storage. And we haven't cleaned out your mom's house yet!"

He had me. My husband was, and I feel like the Fonz when I'm saying this, he was rrrrrr…he was rrrriiiii…

Let's just say that he was correct in his assessment. I know when I'm beaten. He kept all of his boxes. If he has more, I'm keeping my mouth shut.

There's not a lot of stuff left in our house, though. It's good for prospective buyers not to think that you've lost your mind when they see all the seasons of *Buffy the Vampire Slayer* that you own.

Uh, not that I own any. I'm just using that as an example.

So in the past week, my husband and I have packed, cleaned, painted, and straightened. We've pulled out the "good comforter" to put on the bed. We've fixed every little stupid thing around here that has bugged us for years—but obviously not enough to make us fix it before planning to move.

You know what?

Our home looks really good.

Really, really good.

Our dang house looks so good that a part of me is wondering why we're moving. Now everything is the way I always wanted it.

I know we're not the only people who do this. Years ago, our former next-door neighbors installed a new kitchen floor. I was so happy for the wife because she had wanted one for years. A month later, a "For Sale" sign appeared.

I've decided that when we move, we are going to fix things up to our liking in our new house fairly quickly.

I'm going to use the good comforter all the time if I want to. The special glasses and tablecloths—they're coming out of hiding, too. Heck, I might even use them during cookouts.

I must really be losing it. Please disregard that last sentence. I think I hit my head while packing. I will NOT be using my good tablecloths during a cookout.

I'd like to keep writing, but I have to get back to my chores. There's still more to pack away.

Because this stuff really does multiply, you know.

Open House, Schmopen House

After talking with Sandy, our Realtor, we have decided to have an Open House. Actually, we are planning to have a lot of them to increase our chances of selling this place as soon as possible.

So this means a couple of things: first, we need to keep the house clean. Really clean. Like "we're not even living here" clean.

The other thing is that we need to be out of here every Sunday that we decide to have one. Why? It's kind of difficult to sell a house when the family that currently owns it is lying sprawled around the family room wearing faded clothes with bleach stains and/or tiny holes in them—the kind that you don't wear around company—watching marathons of *Law & Order*.

As a result, we will be out of the house doing, well, something. And since it's winter, that won't include sitting outside on benches "people watching" or any other outdoor activities. I'm thinking we'll be seeing a lot of movies and eating out at a lot of restaurants.

The one thing we have discovered about preparing our home for the first Open House is that we are really overthinking what needs to be done. We assumed we would have to paint the whole place. We thought we would have to get new carpet. We thought we would have to fix up the basement so that it looked like a place where folks could gather, rather than a dungeon where we send any door-to-door solicitors.

We didn't have to do any of this.

Sandy explained that our walls looked decent and that we should just give a carpet allowance to the buyer. That way, whoever buys the house can get what they want.

This really made sense to me. When Brad and I were first looking for the home we are in now, we looked at a lot of townhouses. I remember one that touted it had "brand new carpet throughout." We were excited to look at that one because we had already seen a house that had burnt-orange colored carpet in one bedroom and lime-green shag in another. (This was the first time we saw something in a house that we couldn't "unsee." It was hideous. I don't think it even looked good when it was first put down in 1974.)

New carpet sounds great, doesn't it?

Yeah, it does.

Unless, of course, that new carpet is really dark brown.

And it was all through the house.

There may be folks who like dark brown carpet, but I'm not one of them.

When my husband saw it, he said, "Wow. My parents had dark brown carpet in our house. But that was in 1973."

That's why I could understand how it was smarter to give the buyer money toward new flooring. So if he or she wanted dark brown carpeting, they could put it here themselves. But I'm not taking the blame.

Before we had our first Open House, I read a lot of articles on what you could do to help make your house more appealing. I decided that I would bake chocolate chip cookies on the morning of the Open House. Sandy could offer visitors fresh-baked treats. The smell would bring back good memories for potential buyers. Or as my husband said, "Who has bad memories connected with cookies? It's just not possible."

I thought we had this all together. But here's what happened on the morning of our first Open House…

I baked cookies. But I realized that I had to do this much earlier than I planned because I had to get the kitchen spotless again. So guess what? The smell of the cookies had dissipated by the time I had finished cleaning. I reacted as I usually do when faced with this kind of situation.

I freaked out.

"What are we going to do?" I screeched to my husband. "The cookie smell is gone!"

I remembered reading that if you boiled water with cinnamon sticks in it, it would give a smell like freshly baked goodies.

It wouldn't smell like chocolate chip cookies. But it would smell like something good. I would do that.

I spent the next hour boiling water with cinnamon sticks. Then I tried to get the smell to waft through the house by carrying the pot of water around the first floor.

This was probably not a good idea.

"Don't do that!" Brad said. "If you spill it on yourself, we won't have to figure out what we're doing for the rest of the day because we'll be in the Emergency Room!"

I dumped out the water. Then I cleaned the pot, dried it, and put it away. Then I realized that if I threw the cinnamon sticks away in the trash, folks would see them there and know that I was trying to make them feel good by smelling Grandma's apple pie. They most likely wouldn't have, but as I said, I was freaking out and had begun imagining what the folks—who weren't even at our house yet—would be thinking about me and/or my house.

In retrospect, you know what they were probably thinking? "Mmmmm...free cookies!"

Brad took out the trash, even though it just had cinnamon sticks in it.

I looked around the house. It looked good. It smelled good. Now we just needed the right buyer to come by.

Then I noticed that the dish drainer looked awful.

"It's fine," Brad said.

"It's got soap scum on it," I yelled.

"No one is going to notice that at all—and it's a stain. It won't come off. I've scrubbed it," he replied.

"What if they see it and think, 'What other gross stuff is going on in this place?' Then they won't buy the house, and we won't get our new home. And all because of a dish drainer."

It was too late. It was time to go. We had to vacate the premises.

Just before I walked out the door, I grabbed the soap-scummy dish drainer and shoved it into the oven.

I hope no one checks to see if the oven works. Because instead of thinking that we have a dirty home, they would just think that we are nuts.

My Husband, the "Magic" Man

There are some things in life that just don't mix: oil and water, gas and a match, ketchup and ice cream (unless you're into that sort of thing—gag).

I've discovered a new one: my husband and the Magic Eraser.

If you don't know what the Magic Eraser is, let me tell you about it. It's this cleaning thing (yes, I'm sure those are the exact words used by the product's marketing department) by Mr. Clean. It's white and kind of spongy, and is shaped much like an eraser.

And it's magic. Really.

You wet it and wipe a black mark on your wall—POOF! It's gone. No sticky cleaners to use. Nothing. It's just gone.

It reminds me of what my late grandmother used to say about the fax machine: "I don't understand how it does it; it's like voodoo."

Since we've gotten our house together to be shown, we've cleaned it so much. In fact, we've probably cleaned it more in the last week than we have in the last decade.

(And if you're my mother-in-law, and you're reading this, please disregard that previous sentence. It's lies, all lies. Our house is always sparkling clean. I swear.)

The one thing about getting your house *so* clean is that you start to notice things that you normally wouldn't.

Here's the part where my husband and the Magic Eraser come in.

Brad began using the Magic Eraser on spots that were obvious, like fingerprints or a smear here or there.

Now he's begun to get a little batty with it.

He's a man on a mission…

I came downstairs the other day—and it was on a day when there were people scheduled to look at the house—and he suddenly came walking by, eraser in hand.

"Honey, what are you doing?" I asked. "We're getting ready to go."

"Just a minute. Look at all these spots on the wall. I've got to get rid of them," he replied.

I didn't see a thing. But his face was about one millimeter from the wall, so he must have been able to see things that I couldn't.

Or he's developed superpowers and can see into the very fiber of the walls. The way he's been cleaning, that's more likely what has happened.

So we're getting ready to leave to have lunch and see a movie. He got the Magic Eraser again.

"Wait a minute, there's a mark here on the door," he said, scrubbing away.

Then he saw—GASP—a tiny spot near the doorknob.

On the basement door.

Where no one is going to look anyway.

(I can guarantee that there are no spots of any kind on our walls, doors, doorframes, ceilings, closet doors, or cabinet doors. At least none that I've seen or that my husband and his superpowers and trusty Magic Eraser have seen.)

He kept Magic Erasering the walls until I told him that if we didn't leave immediately, we would not only miss lunch and the movie, but we would look like goofballs when the people who were coming to view the home walked in.

Can you imagine that? We'd look completely OCD. Or like we were cleaning up from a crime scene—neither of which makes a good impression on potential buyers.

By this time, our house was even more sparkling clean than it was five minutes before, when we were initially leaving. And he had used this particular Magic Eraser until it was all scrunchy looking. It had seen better days. He threw it away, and we got ready to leave.

First, though, he had to run upstairs to get something. And it's a good thing he did.

In his quest to keep our house looking as clean as possible, my husband had taken all of our dirty laundry down to the basement early that morning.

Except for one thing.

A pair of dirty underwear that he dropped on the steps.

Where anyone viewing the house would have not only seen them, but also had to step over them.

And I don't know about you, but seeing someone else's dirty underwear doesn't exactly make me want to buy a house.

The checklist we consult before leaving the house will now include, "Make sure there's no dirty underwear on the floor."

Because that's one thing the Magic Eraser can't get rid of.

Take My House, Please—We're Tired of Keeping It So Clean!

For those of you who have never sold a home, let me enlighten you. Do you know what the most difficult part of it all is?

It's not waiting for a contract.

It's not having Open Houses.

It's not even rushing out on a moment's notice after the real estate office calls saying, "Michele, there's someone right outside your door who wants to see the house. Can they?"

I expected all that.

What I didn't expect, though, is how hard it is to keep the dang place clean.

I've already explained how we've cleared the clutter out of our home so that people can, uh, actually see it when they come to look. You know what I've discovered? You see a lot more dust when there's not as much clutter.

I'm dusting and vacuuming our house more than I probably have in all the time that we've owned it.

(Unless, that is, you're a prospective buyer, in which case, I've always dusted every room and vacuumed the entire carpet. Every day. For over a decade. You could eat off this floor. But please don't, because that would make me have to vacuum again.)

My husband, who's obsessed with the Magic Eraser, said to me the other day, "I can't wait until we sell this house so that we can be slobs again!"

Let me clarify: we aren't slobs. We never leave plates full of food sitting in rooms. We never have bug infestations.

But if we let some laundry pile up, it isn't a big deal.

Until, that is, we put our house on the market.

The thing about selling your house is that, as strange as it sounds, you have to make it look cozy, so that people can imagine themselves living there. But you don't want them to have any idea that you actually live there now.

Confused? Join the club.

For example, in the morning, you brush your teeth, right? Well, now you've had to spit in the sink. And people who are looking to buy your house don't want to think about you having spit in the sink that morning. They don't want to know that you've taken a shower or used the toilet.

So just rinsing the sink out isn't good enough. Every day, after we've all had our showers, etc., I attack the bathrooms, and clean them up. I don't want a couple of water spots to deter someone from putting their name on the dotted line.

I'm cleaning our storm door every single day. Do you know why? Because our dogs love to look outside during the day, and when doing so, they push their snotty little noses up against the glass.

Someone who might want to buy our home could think, "Ewwww…dog nose prints. There's no way I'm buying this house now!"

All right   they probably wouldn't say that. But I've developed this habit of trying to get inside the heads of possible buyers and make everything look pleasing to them. Which, granted, is pretty insane.

I also make sure that there are no stains, smells, or remnants from our dogs. There's no dog hair on the floors or on the furniture because we are vacuuming each day.

We hide the dog bowls.

We hide the treats.

We hide the toys.

There is absolutely no evidence of our stinky, furry friends anywhere. Keeping the house dog-hair free, when the dog who sheds most is black, has not been the easiest thing to do.

You know what else is hard to do? Eat. I mean this. Because we can't be right in the middle of cooking a meal, eating it, or—gasp—be cleaning up if someone wants to come and see the house.

We've eaten so much carryout in the last couple of weeks that when this is all over, I think I'll eat nothing but fresh vegetables for a month.

So we've been doing our best to eat healthful foods. Then we take the plastic containers they came in, throw them in the trash, and take the trash outside.

And don't give me any stuff about how I'm ruining the environment and adding to the landfills. I've got enough stress in my life right now and adding guilt will probably make my head explode.

Or it could push me over the edge and cause me not to care about how clean my house is. I may not make the bed using the "good" comforter. Heck, I may not make the bed at all.

Perhaps I'll begin to spit in the sink and leave remnants of toothpaste so that, like a dog marking its territory, buyers will know that I live here.

I could leave dirty dishes in the sink, ignore the ring in the tub, and let the dust pile up. Then I'd put out a sign, encouraging visitors to write their names in the aforementioned dust to let me know that they had been here.

I'll let dirty laundry pile up. I'll leave mail on the table. I'll encourage family members to stop flushing the toilets.

Okay. I have now successfully grossed myself out.

Who am I kidding? I know I couldn't do that. Even if we're tired of being "so clean."

Now if you'll excuse me, I have to go find the Magic Eraser.

Out of House, Out of (My) Mind

We are really motivated to sell our house. As I said, we have to get a contract on our present house in order to purchase our dream home.

We are so motivated that in the last 10 weeks we have done the following:

We have boarded our three dogs—Snoopy, Rose, and Steve (they insist that we use pseudonyms as they don't want their doggie friends to make fun of them)—at our vets for the entire weekend. We take them in on Friday and bring them home on Monday. Why? Because having three dogs jumping all over folks who want to look at our home is an easy way to get them to leave—especially if they don't like dogs. (We think that by the time this is all over, we'll have either funded a long, tropical vacation for our vet and his extended family or will have put his kids through college. Or both.)

During this time, we have had eight—yes, eight!—Sunday Open Houses. No, this is not the norm.

But we are willing to do anything necessary to get this house sold, especially in a tough market.

We have had to be out of our house every Sunday for most of the day. What we discovered, though, is that we also have to be out of the house for most of the day on Saturday. Seems that a lot of people want to look at a house privately—as in not during the Open House—so we aim to please.

Because it's winter, we haven't been able to spend a lot of the time away from our house outside enjoying nature. It's freezing out. We have spent a lot of time at the movies.

So far, we have seen 10—count 'em, 10—movies.

Before this, I don't think I'd seen 10 movies in the movie theater in the last five years.

We have eaten out so much, I have gained seven pounds. My husband and my stepdad? They haven't gained any weight *and* they always order dessert. This is *so* not fair!!! How is this happening? It's really ticking me off.

You know what else happens in the winter because of the cold? Snow. When we came out of the movie theater one day, we were greeted with three inches of snow on the ground. I freaked out. Not because we're selling the house, though.

I freaked out because I'm a Baltimorean, and we all freak out during snow—even if it's just one inch. We run to the grocery stores and buy bread, milk, eggs, and toilet paper. Why? I don't know. We just do it. In the summer, we eat steamed crabs, and in the winter, we freak out at even the possibility of snow. Sometimes we even close the schools when it hasn't even started snowing yet.

But I digress…

I have gained some usable skills during this time—like learning where every single bathroom is in every movie theater, mall, and shopping center within 20 miles of our home. I've learned how to be ready at a moment's notice and to get three dogs, my stepdad, and piles of paper for my current writing projects packed up and in the car, ready to leave so that someone can come and look at our house.

Brad and I have learned to be really flexible—like the time that we ordered carryout food on the way home from a movie, then got a call from our Realtor saying that people wanted to look at our home. We asked the carryout place if we could change our order from

Michele Wojciechowski

"to go" to " for here." We then took our time eating because we knew that if we got home early, we would just have to wait in the car.

Which brings me to how we have, on occasion, had to stalk our own house.

There have been times when we have gone out of our house for an hour after we got a call that someone wanted to see it. When we arrived back home, folks were still inside. So we parked our car in one of the Visitor Parking spots in our development (each home gets two spots, and we have to leave them open for the people who come to look at our home). We then watch and wait for them to finish.

One time, we sat in our car with the heat on and watched people talk outside for an entire hour.

Then there was the time that I had to get the dogs and my stepdad into the car (because it was during the day and during the week while my husband was at work) and away from the house. Since I work from home, this fun job belongs to me. I wouldn't mind sitting in the car with my stepdad for an hour, talking. But the dogs run back and forth along the backseat, whining and barking. They look like they are having a doggie frat party in the car.

I can't simply park in a Visitor's Spot; it would draw too much attention. So I do the next best thing.

I drive up the street and sit in the parking lot of a local grocery store.

The last time I had to do this, the dogs were particularly hyper, and my stepdad was yelling at them to calm down—which doesn't work at all.

Then it began to snow...

Of course, now I had to go *into* the grocery store and buy bread, milk, eggs, and toilet paper.

If we don't sell this house soon, I'm going to end up in a mental institution.

All Our House Is a Stage...

After we had many Open Houses, Sandy, our Realtor, came over. The point was to try and figure out if there was something else we could do to attract folks to our home.

It's clean.

It's pet free.

When folks came to see it, it's occupant free.

Sandy had an idea. We were going to "stage" the dining room. She said, "It's called 'staging' for a reason. It's not real life."

The whole point of staging is that you do things to the house or a room that you would never do in real life.

We've already been staging parts of the house. For example, we put fresh flowers in a vase in the living room and more on the breakfast bar. While we do get fresh flowers once in a while, we don't put them all over the house. And, unlike the flowers we put out for staging, when we do it in real life, they aren't perfect.

After a week, they begin to wilt or the water gets slimy and smells bad, so we get rid of them.

The flowers in our staged house, though, are sweet smelling and perfectly shaped and brilliantly colored.

They are weird.

We've already changed our dining room. Our regular dining room table is a bit large for the room, so we put it into storage, and, instead, have a round table in the dining room, covered in a beautiful floor-length tablecloth.

We never sit at that table.

We never eat at that table.

Before the house was up for sale, that table had never been in this room.

We thought it made the dining room look, well, roomier. But Sandy had another idea.

"Trust me," she said. "This is going to seem weird, but just trust me."

I am so desperate to sell our home. I am tired of going to the movies, and I long for a weekend where

I can just prop my feet up and watch mindless TV all day long.

If she told me that I had to paint myself blue and run around in the front yard in order to sell the house, I'd be out front looking like Smurfette.

What we ended up doing was almost as strange.

We took out the fake dining table. Sandy placed a carved, wooden plant stand in the room against a wall. She put a lamp on it.

Then she put a chair next to it. She said we could leave our corner china cabinet where it was.

"This looks ridiculous," I said.

"I know. But it's staged. Just trust me," Sandy said.

"Who in their right mind would put just a chair in the dining room against the wall like this? This looks out of place," I said.

"It doesn't matter if people would actually do it or not," Sandy said. "Trust me."

So we did.

And guess what happened?

During the next Open House, Sandy said that folks came into the dining room, looked up at the chandelier, and said something like, "Oh, look at the pretty lights. Do you know what we could do? We could put a table in here and make it a dining room!"

Are you kidding me?!

Of course they can! It *is* the dining room!

I can't believe prospective buyers are getting all excited because they've come up with a brand new idea for the dining room—they'll make it a dining room!

Just so I'm clear on this, the "idea" of a table in the dining room is okay.

Having the table itself in there—not so much.

Table or no table—makes no difference to me.

Until we get a contract, you'll find us eating carryout in the family room.

Our House Is Almost Gone
and So Are Our Minds

We've done everything our Realtor has asked.

We've painted or didn't...

We've made it look like we didn't have pets...

We've used so many Magic Erasers to keep the place clean that we should have taken out stock in the company.

The stress is getting to me.

Some days when we put out new flowers for staging, I yell things like "You want a fake house? I'll give you a fake house!"

Overall, I'm pleased with myself because I haven't completely lost it yet. But there's still time.

One week after our "staging the dining room" Open House, we have an offer on our home.

The buyer even offered our asking price.

I should be thrilled. But one small request put me over the edge.

The buyer wants us to pay his closing costs.

In the broader scheme of things, this isn't a lot of money.

This isn't a big deal.

People pay closing costs for their buyers all the time.

For some reason, though, I totally lost it anyway.

"That's it!" I yelled. "I'm done with all of this! We do everything we're supposed to, and everyone is screwing us! The people we're buying from have us paying more than we offered, and now this person wants us to give him more money! Everyone gets what they want! Closing costs? Sure, let's pay them. Let's pay more for the house we're buying! Why don't we hire a band and little girls to throw rose petals at their feet when they move in while we're at it?"

I was crying by this time. When I looked at my husband, his mouth was open, and he was looking all bug-eyed.

"I know you think I'm crazy!" I sputtered. "I know you think I'm crazy! But I don't care! I'm sick of all of this!"

I then put my head down on the breakfast bar and sobbed.

At this point, Super Realtor Sandy, who will definitely go straight to real estate heaven after dealing with us (um, okay, me), looked at me and softly said, "But Michele, you'll be getting your dream home, right?"

"That's not the point," I wailed.

But that really is the point. We are getting our dream home. I just want all the stress to be over.

I blew my nose, wiped my eyes, and said, "All right. We'll pay the closing costs."

Sandy said that she often sees buyers and sellers lose it over something minor. Some scream. Some curse. Others, like me, cry and temporarily refuse to pay closing costs. Then they pull it together and continue.

Tonight, we sign the contract. We are on our way.

Oh. My. God.

We Sold Our House!
We Sold Our House!
We Sold Our House!

Woo hoo!

Yahoo!

Yee-hah!

We sold our house!

Can you tell that I'm a tad bit excited about it?

Even though we're psyched about moving, I have to admit that it's slightly bittersweet. We've had a lot of fun here.

After Brad and I became engaged, we began looking for our first home. We had gotten listings from our real estate agent, and we decided to drive around and look at the homes before we made appointments to see them.

If we didn't like the exterior of the house or the area or the street, what was the point of going in?

(One of the houses we looked at had siding that was the color of, as my family so eloquently put it, "baby poop yellow." That one was out.)

When we pulled up in front of one townhome, I noticed the house had a bay window.

"Oh my God!" I exclaimed. "I would have a window seat."

"This is the house. I know this is the house. I can just feel it."

Brad replied, "Let's wait until we see the inside. Don't get too set on this house yet."

Mr. Rational struck again. I, having finally gotten excited about a house, became infuriated.

We pulled over into a parking lot, where I cried and told him that he was killing my dreams, I knew this was the house, how could he be so crass, blah, blah, blah…

Did I mention that I had recently begun my free-lance writing business? Oh, and we were planning our wedding, too. So I wasn't stressed out or anything.

Years later, we still joke about pulling into that parking lot and our argument about him being a "dream-killer."

That house ended up being "the one." A couple of months after we moved in, we got a neighbor's relative—let's call him "Fred"—to install another phone line in my office. The problem was our walls were so fireproofed that every time the guy drilled a hole inside the wall and pulled out the gigantic bit, he couldn't fish the line down because the stuff in the wall would close around it.

He spent hours here and burned up a drill bit. The house stank.

That evening, the smell was everywhere in the house. It smelled like something was burning. Having no idea if something could be smoldering in the wall, we decided to call Fred.

"I don't think anything's wrong," he said. "But if you're worried, get some baby powder, and pour it into the hole." He hadn't been able to get the line run yet, and there was a hole in my office wall.

There I stood, squeezing baby powder into a hole in my wall. Puff, puff, puff. Now the house smelled like something burning *and* baby powder.

We figured that the smell would be gone by morning, so we went to bed.

When we got up, the smell was worse. We knew that something had to be smoldering in that wall.

I called 911.

"I don't have an emergency. I just need to talk to the fire department about a smell," I said. The operator gave me the dispatcher's number.

"We don't have a fire. We just have a burnt smell. I don't know what to do," I explained. The dispatcher assured me that they should check it out anyway. He would make sure to let the fire department know that we had no fire, just a smell.

That guy must have left out the part about us not having a fire in the wall.

Soon a fire truck, sirens blaring, came screaming up in front of our house.

The neighbors got to know us really fast.

A couple of young firefighters, brandishing axes so that they could chop through the wall to get to the fire (which didn't exist), came running through our front door and up the stairs to my office.

"But it's just a smell!" I yelled.

The firefighters were not happy. I explained to one that I had told dispatch it was only a smell.

There was no fire.

They left.

Just in case, I squeezed more baby powder into the wall. By the next day, the smell was gone.

I think our neighbors are going to miss us and good times like that.

Where Did All This Stuff Come From?

After we got the contract on our townhome, I thought that the major stress was over. We had a buyer, so now we could get ready for glorious days in our new home.

Wrong. More stress was just beginning.

Or at least the packing was. And, as I've discovered, packing is pretty dang stressful.

Over the years, I've referred to myself as a recovering packrat. But by the stuff I've looked through and packed already, I still have a long way to go.

I keep asking my husband, "Where did all this stuff come from?"

He says that it just looks like a lot because we're packing it.

Because I believe highly in the power of deluding myself, I agree with him.

Here's an example for you: we have a small—and I mean really small—corner china cabinet in the dining room. There's not a lot of stuff in there. I figured I could fit it in a box or two.

Oh no. It took me five boxes to get everything packed. FIVE!

This gets me thinking that if it took me five boxes for this little piece of furniture, it will probably take me about 7,000 to pack the stuff in my bedroom closet.

And I don't even own a lot of shoes!

How is this possible?

While I just had a theory before—that this stuff was multiplying at night while my husband and I slept—now I'm sure of it. Our stuff is procreating—especially the magazines and paperwork and other pieces of stuff in my office. And the knickknacks and CDs and books.

Especially the books...

I may have had two bestsellers sitting on a shelf in the basement.

They got to know each other.

Their spines touched.

And when two books fall in love...

Then there were three, then four, then 10, now 1,000.

Are you buying this? Nope, me neither.

Because we're in a bit of a rush to get everything packed (last time we bought a house, it took two months for us to settle. Now, it's done in about three or four weeks), my husband keeps saying, "Don't worry about it. We'll go through everything when we get to the new house, and we'll get rid of a lot of stuff."

Boy, is he the optimist. I mean, he knows that I recently bought a hammock. If I have the choice between spending a nice summer evening unpacking boxes or reading while lying in a hammock, which do you think I'll choose?

I have had many friends say, "Make sure you unpack as soon as you get into the house. If you don't, you'll end up like us, with boxes in the basement that haven't been opened in 10 years."

So many people have said similar things to me that I feel like it's something we should do—just leave a bunch of boxes in the basement, hidden away so that I can discover them in a couple of decades and exclaim "Hey, I thought we had gotten rid of this!"

As I said, we have a lot of stuff. As a result, we've needed a lot of boxes. Today, though, it's not as easy to get boxes as it used to be because most grocery stores break them down as soon as they unpack them.

And I absolutely refuse to buy boxes.

It's not because I'm cheap. God knows we've put out money during this whole process—on everything from eating out to the tons of money that our vet is going to get when we settle up our bill for boarding the dogs. (I think my vet should thank me when he and his wife are sipping drinks with little umbrellas in them on some tropical island. Remember, I paid for that.)

Everyone close to me has become a "box stalker." My husband is snatching them from work, my friend has gotten some from a pharmacy, and I've tracked some down at a wholesale club and a local restaurant.

Our living room is full of boxes, and our dogs are freaking out. There's still so much stuff to pack, and I've got deadlines to meet. There are still papers to sign, and utilities to transfer.

And people tell me this is one of the happiest times of my life...

I think I'll go unpack my hammock.

The Many Joys and Surprises of Packing

I once interviewed a wise woman from an Army background. She told me that there's a saying in the Army: War is hell. Moving is a close second.

Amen.

As we continue the seemingly never-ending saga of packing to move, we begin this episode with my soon-to-be-no-longer neighbor Adam.

Last week, he brought over an enormous box. "I know you needed boxes, so I bought a lawn mower," he said.

I will miss him and his family being right next door.

My husband and I have discovered many surprises in the midst of packing.

Like deep red, touch-up paint for my 1986 Chevy Nova.

We got rid of that car five years ago.

Or the empty piece of cardboard from a roll of tape.

Neither one of us can figure out why we kept that one.

And some bottle of mysterious, unmarked cleaner that, well, stinks.

My friend Patti came over for a few hours to help me pack. We've known each other since high school. Despite this, I've discovered that just when you think you know a person, you find out that you don't.

Patti could be a professional packer.

I'm serious.

Patti packed paper plates, pens and pencils, and piles of paper in boxes faster than, as my late Mom would have said, Grant took Richmond. But she had a grace and skill to it.

She held boxes up and said things like, "This is heavier on one side than the other. Have to fix that."

What? I haven't been doing that at all. I've just filled a box and then made sure that it wasn't so heavy that it would take a small army of elephants to drag it outside. I'd tape it and mark it.

That was as far as I would go.

But not Patti. For her, there was a science to it.

Everything was packed at a good weight with a good balance. Patti had done them perfectly.

Perfect Patti.

Perfect Patti makes me sick.

I said to her, "You should have helped me when I started packing. Things would be so much better."

Perfect Patti paused, then said, "Perhaps."

My stepdad, Efficient Ed, can fit three shelves of books into one box. He sits there with patience and, like a skilled puzzle-putter-together guy (yes, this is a word), he moves them around until he gets maximum bookage in each box.

Ed's excellent.

Ed's exceptional.

Ed's extraordinary.

Michele Wojciechowski

Then there's me.

While I was wrapping some glassware in bubble wrap, my husband said, "You're putting the bubbles on the outside. Shouldn't they go near the thing you're wrapping?"

Well, I'd never thought of that before. But since we were on a tight deadline to get all this stuff packed, I did the mature, adult thing.

I went to my computer to look it up.

Turns out that more than 50 percent of people are using bubble wrap incorrectly. Guess who else was? Yup. Me.

A colleague told me that when you wrap fine art, you want the bubble side facing out.

However, when you wrap your collection of jelly jars featuring the comic book characters Archie, Betty, Jughead, and Veronica—bubbles in.

Great. Now there are specific scenarios for when the bubbles go in, and when they go out. Suddenly, we're doing the Bubble Wrap Hokey Pokey—you put your bubbles in, you put your bubbles out...

Another friend, Radical Rosie, suggested that I take all my bubble wrap, put it on the floor, and step all over it.

Pop, pop, poppity, pop, pop, pop!

Yeah, it would be fun for a few minutes—or a few hours—but I don't have that kind of time right now.

And I'd have nothing to pack my jelly jars in.

And they would get broken.

And the sight of Betty's chipped face would make me sad.

That woman was right: War may be hell, but moving—and the packing that goes with it—is definitely a close second.

Let's Get a Move On...

Three weeks after we accepted the contract on our townhome, we had our closings.

See, when you are buying a house and selling a house at the same time, you get to go to two closings in one day. It's just so much fun.

Not.

Especially when your last name happens to be Wojciechowski, which you get to sign about 7 billion times.

What's even more fun is that you get to sign documents that are ridiculous. Like the one that says there is no lead paint in our house. Considering that our townhome was built in the '80s, and lead paint wasn't being used anymore, it was ridiculous to have to sign the lead paint paperwork.

When I asked Sandy, our Realtor, about it, she said, "I know; I know. Just sign it anyway."

So we did.

In a few short hours, we went from owning our townhome to owning our dream home. We took Sandy and our mortgage broker, Mary, out to a celebratory lunch. Afterwards, Sandy gave Brad and me house-warming gifts. For me, a basket full of relaxation bath products. For Brad, a few boxes of Magic Erasers…

She knows us so well.

That evening, our soon-to-be-former next-door neighbors, Adam and Kristen, along with my Aunt Kathie and Uncle Tom, helped us load up our cars, two jeeps, and a pickup truck with stuff from our home. We decided to move a bunch of boxes the night before the big move. We thought this would save us time.

We were wrong.

In retrospect, I think what we should have done was finish packing the stuff in the basement. (Yes, we still had some stuff to pack. I told you that it kept multiplying.)

We got up at dawn the next morning. Everything was ready to go except for some stuff in the basement.

We had hired professional movers, and we figured that they would load all of the furniture into the truck first, then go back for the boxes of smaller stuff.

We were wrong.

This is not how movers move stuff—at least not our movers. At 7 a.m., they knocked on the door and walked right down to the basement.

My husband and I looked at each other, sheer panic in our eyes.

"Hey, aren't you going to load all of the furniture first?" I asked them.

"No," the one guy answered. "We start in the basement and empty that out, then move to the first floor, then finish with the second floor."

Brad and I ran down to the basement and began throwing stuff into boxes. We weren't making sure they were balanced. We weren't writing anything on the sides. We were just cramming stuff in.

I think if I had listened closely, I would have heard my packing-wizard friend, Perfect Patti, scream in dismay.

Michele Wojciechowski

The two of us were tossing everything into boxes as fast as we could. We were packing with the intensity of Lucy and Ethel in the episode of *I Love Lucy* where they work in the chocolate factory and the conveyer belt goes haywire.

I would have given anything to be working in a chocolate factory rather than packing in our basement. It would have been much more fun to cram candy in my mouth than to shove everything from tools to games to possibly empty paint cans into boxes.

At the time, I had only one thing on my mind: we needed this house empty. As soon as possible.

The magnificent movers joined in and then there were five of us flinging stuff. (Okay, truth be told, two of us were flinging stuff and the other three were professionally packing it.)

The movers worked for the rest of the day, and we helped where we could. In only two trips, they moved 95 percent of the stuff we had accumulated in the 12 years we lived in this home.

The movers were finished by 5 p.m.

And so were we.

As I looked back at my house for the last time, I got a little choked up. But I knew it was time to move on. Our work here was done.

At our dream home, though, our work was just beginning.

Okay, I Give Up—What Does This Switch Do?

As we've settled into our new home, Brad and I have put new contact paper in all the kitchen cabinets, decided where to put our furniture, and figured out how to turn the dang lights on.

We have also been playing a new game called "What Does This Switch Do?"

Since we're getting used to our new home, we still don't know what the many switches in a particular room do, unless it's one with only one or two switches.

Next to our front door, there are five switches. In the short time we've been here, we have flipped all of them on and off in an attempt to turn on one particular light.

Click, click.

Click, click.

And I still can't get used to them.

I know; my mom would tell me to be patient.

But sometimes you feel really stupid having to turn five switches on and off until you pick the right one.

I thought that I could temporarily label them. You know what, though? Then everyone who comes over would know that we (meaning I) couldn't figure out what switches did what.

Where are a bunch of little kids when you need them?

If we had kids, I could do this and then blame it on them. "Oh, we marked that because we're teaching little Johnny and Sally how to turn off the lights to save energy."

We would be seen as good, educating, environmentally concerned parents.

Another option is that we could say it's because we are teaching the dogs to turn them on and off, but I know no one will buy that.

And that's just in the front of the house.

I went to turn on the lights in the kitchen the other day and successfully turned on the garbage disposal.

Luckily, that awful grinding noise tipped me off right away, and I turned it off. Then I found the correct switch.

We also have a garage door opener, which I've never had before. So far, I've remembered to push that button each time I'm driving into or out of the garage. I haven't forgotten and crashed into the garage door.

So far, so good.

Although I *have* pulled too close to the freezer in the garage. Okay, my husband is going to read this, so I might as well tell the truth: I've, uh, "tapped" it with the car bumper a couple of times.

Hey, cut me some slack—it's not like I've dented it or anything.

And just to make sure I don't, my husband is moving the freezer to another area of the garage this weekend.

But I digress…

Every day, I hit the wrong switch to turn on the light over the kitchen table. Instead, it turns on another light in the kitchen.

Every. Single. Time.

It goes like this: Click. Wrong light.

I utter a nasty word.

Click. Turn on right light.

Click. Turn wrong light back off.

I need a faster learning curve. This is driving me nuts.

I don't need this stress.

Remember, I've got enough with the 7 kabillion boxes I haven't unpacked yet.

I go to a room to start working in it, and hit the switch.

Click, click.

Click, click.

ARGH!

Maybe I will mark what switch does what. At least until the housewarming party, that is...

We're Finally Unpacking, and
We Can't Find Anything

As I write this, we've been in our new home for a few weeks.

My stepdad got his hair cut today, and Sonny, our hairdresser, asked if we were finished unpacking yet.

Bah ha ha ha ha ha ha ha…

He is such a funny man.

Suffice it to say we're not even close to being finished. There are still boxes in every single room of this house.

Family and friends are asking when they can come over to see the place.

Again, I say, Bah ha ha ha ha ha ha ha…

How about sometime between now and when hell freezes over? I think I should be done unpacking by then.

If anyone ever tells you that once you're in your new home, the stress is over, take note: these people are lying.

I have to admit, though, that we have been playing many new fun and interesting games since the unpacking began.

Like the one called "Find the Scissors."

We need a pair of scissors.

We have about a dozen.

We can't find any.

Not. A. One.

"Would you have marked that on the box?" asked Brad.

Uh, no. Do you know why? Because I was lucky I could mark "kitchen" or "bedroom" on the 7 kabillion boxes that we moved here. If I'd marked down everything that was in them, I'd still be sitting in our old house.

My husband is a funny, funny man.

I finally found a box with eight pairs of crafty scissors in them.

I was desperate. I took a pair that made waves instead of straight cuts and began to tackle the paper and tape wrapped around the wicker furniture for our front porch.

The wavy scissors did the trick. Although I don't think that the recycle guy will care if our cardboard is pretty or not.

My husband did finally locate one—just one— pair of scissors. I put the craft scissors away.

The next game we played was called "Where's a Phone?"

"Would you have marked it on a box?" asked my husband, who has obviously lost just as many brain cells as I have during this move.

"There will be a phone in a box marked 'bedroom' or 'kitchen,' and that's all the clues I can give you," I replied.

Of course, we have about 50 boxes marked either "bedroom" or "kitchen."

"Why don't you call the phone? Then you'll hear it ringing, and we can find it," said my stepdad.

Hmmm…that would have been a good idea. IF THE PHONE WAS HOOKED UP IN THE FIRST PLACE!!!

Gasp. Sputter. Snort...

My stepdad, much like my husband and me, has also lost brain power during the move.

We all went to bed that night not having found a phone. But as it got later, and we got more and more tired, we just didn't care.

If anyone wanted to call, they could leave a message. That's what voicemail was for.

The next day, we found a phone. In fact, we found a few of them. Yee-hah!

Then we had to find the phone jacks. Which were, of course, hidden behind many, many boxes.

The other night, I woke up before four in the morning. I decided to read.

I turned on the lamp on my nightstand.

Crackle.

Then darkness.

The bulb had burned out.

"Do you know where the light bulbs are?" my partially sleeping husband groaned.

"I have no idea," I answered. "Never mind. I'll just lie here and try to go back to sleep."

With that, he rolled over, turned on his lamp, and slinked down under the covers to hide from the light.

I smiled and opened my book.

Even when you're moving, true love is the one thing that, if you've already got it, you can always find.